MORE
WOULD YOU RATHER?

Have bad teeth OR bad eyesight?

FOUR HUNDRED AND SIXTY-FIVE MORE
PROVOCATIVE QUESTIONS TO GET TEENAGERS TALKING

Read a road map OR actually pull over and

DOUG FIELDS

Live during OR be alive when Jesus

Have an arranged marriage OR never marry at all?

Laugh OR make others laugh?

Be on stage OR backstage?

Teach like Jesus OR live like Jesus?

Be a missionary OR China?

ZONDERVAN™
GRAND RAPIDS, MICHIGAN 49530 USA

Youth Specialties
www.YouthSpecialties.com

More Would You Rather
Copyright © 2004 by Doug Fields

Youth Specialties Books, 300 South Pierce Street, El Cajon, CA
92020, are published by Zondervan, 5300 Patterson Avenue SE, Grand
Rapids, MI 49530

Editorial direction by Dave Urbanski
Art direction by Jay Howver
Proofreading by Laura Gross
Interior design by Holly Sharp
Cover design by Proxy
Printed in the United States of America

04 05 06 07 08 09 / DC / 10 9 8 7 6 5 4 3 2 1

This book is dedicated to all the youth workers who have been begging and bugging me for another Would You Rather...? book and promising their students it was on its way.

Many people have contributed to the pile of questions, but special thanks belong to Neely McQueen, Linda Kaye, Dennis Beckner, Ty Mattson, Jack Guiso, Sandy Boyd, Scott Santos, and especially Mark Thrash for all his work sorting, writing, and grossing me out.

Torie, Cody, and Cassie—now that you've got another book to share with your friends, will you please read one of my "real" books? I love you!

INTRODUCTION

THE HISTORY

You might be familiar with the original *Would You Rather...?* It provided a simple tool that youth workers used to catapult students into conversation. It's really amazing that a silly question can be followed by laughter and lead toward a deep, meaningful discussion. I'm still amazed it works.

Personally, I find it humorous when people say "I love your book"...and they're referring to WYR. I've written more than 30 books that are much more substantial (*Purpose Driven Youth Ministry*—400-plus pages and *Your First Two Years in Youth Ministry*—300-pages), but WYR seems to elicit the "I love" exclamation. (Then again, it's the only book I've written that my own children will read. Oh well...)

The fun of using WYR surrounds the many humorous, stupid, and downright disgusting questions. While it's also peppered with an occasional thought-sparker, most students want the gags.

So take your time, mark your favorites, but most of all...have fun and get teenagers talking! These questions really do work. But if you want more than silly questions and desire to know how I use this book to lead to effective discussions, keep reading.

HOW TO USE *MORE WOULD YOU RATHER...?*

IDENTIFY GOALS BEYOND LAUGHTER

Here are some potential goals for using these questions:

1. Get every student talking in a non-threatening environment.
2. Provide questions that students can answer without being "incorrect."
3. Discover how students arrive at their decisions.
4. Challenge and affirm their responses.
5. Help students express and defend their opinions so they develop conviction for what they believe.

If you keep some of these goals in mind, the book can become a significant youth ministry resource.

USE THE RIGHT QUESTION AT THE RIGHT TIME

Some of the questions in *More Would You Rather...?* have no significant value other than to get students involved and moving their lips. Some questions will invite quick answers requiring little to no thought (i.e., "Would you rather have cold feet or sweaty armpits?").

Other questions require more thought and will often spur serious, in-depth responses (i.e., "Would you know your future or change your past?"). Hold these questions for when you want to take your students to a deeper level. Some questions in this book will inspire candid comments about normally guarded feelings. When this happens don't be afraid to set the book down and launch into a deeper follow-up question.

That's the real trick to maximizing *More Would You Rather...?*—building on an answer with follow-up question that comes from *you* and not from the book. For example, you can go deeper by asking, "Why did you choose that?" "How did you arrive at that answer?" "How would it make you feel if you were the only one to answer that way?" and, of course, "Why?" The questions inside these pages really just set the table for deeper questions that will peel back layers and give you glimpses of students' hearts.

CREATE YOUR OWN RULES

You can use these questions any way you choose. You can ask follow-up questions. You can let students challenge each other's answers. You can ask students to explain their answers. You could even ask a student to defend the opposite answer of what she shared.

The only real rule I use is not letting one student dominate and speak for everyone else. There are times when I direct a specific question to quiet students in an effort to get them involved (I guess that's more a tip than a rule). When there is a dominating student I stop reading the questions and have students each call out a number and a name. I then read the question from the number picked and direct the question at the person whose name was called. Then I let others offer their answers before picking another name and number.

PUSH A LITTLE

Don't let your students off the hook too easily. Some questions will cause them to answer "neither, but that's an easy out. Instead challenge your students to answer even when it's weird or uncomfortable. (Or else I'll ask a student to articulate why she choose "neither".)

KEEP IT IN PERSPECTIVE

Remember that listening to your students is more important that finishing a page of questions. If a question sparks a response and opens up meaningful conversation, go with it. Don't worry about getting to the next question no matter how obnoxious the "Read another one!" chants sound.

BE SENSITIVE

Although none of the *More Would You Rather...?* questions are intended to hurt feelings, use wise judgment when asking certain questions. If you have a teenager who has noticeable blemishes, you might not ask a question dealing with a bad case of acne. Think through the questions that will most benefit your students without hurting any feelings.

CODE YOUR FAVORITES

As with the original WYR, you might want to code your favorite questions. I use an **F** for *funny*, a **DD** for questions that will get students to *dig deeper*, and a big **G** for questions that are just plain *GROSS!* I also use an asterisk for questions that result in good discussion.

NO RIGHT OR WRONG ANSWERS

This might be the most insight I can offer: there are no right or wrong answers to these questions. When you toss these questions to your students, make sure you create a safe place for them to share their true feelings (even if their feelings are different than yours). They need to know it's safe to share with you.

HAVE FUN

Use this book as a tool to break down walls and engage students in good conversation, but remember to have fun. Sometimes it will spark a deep conversation... sometimes it won't. If the opportunity to go deeper is there, take it...if not, don't force it and just have fun.

For more than 25 years I have used humor in my ministry to students. I use humor because it's what I respond to personally. I love to laugh and joke around (I decided to follow Christ after hearing a comedian share the gospel). I also use humor because I have seen it break down walls in other people around me. Whether it's gross or silly or wacky or repulsive, humor has a way of bridging the ever-widening gap that separates students from a place where they are open to hearing God's voice.

The best thing about *More Would You Rather...?* is that it gives me, a youth worker, an opportunity to care about a student's opinion. So don't think of these as 465 silly questions; rather think of them as 465 opportunities to listen, 465 chances to make eye-contact, and 465 reasons to love teenagers.

Would you rather be a teenager or a youth worker? I choose youth worker! Thanks for being one, too.

Blessings,

Doug Fields

1   FORGET TO WEAR DEODORANT
    ON A DATE OR ENDURE YOUR
    DATE'S BODY ODOR?

2   BE KISSED BY YOUR MOM IN
    PUBLIC OR YELLED AT BY YOUR
    DAD IN PRIVATE?

3   SQUISH A ROACH WITH YOUR
    BARE FEET OR A SPIDER WITH
    YOUR HAND?

4   EAT WORMS OR HAVE WORMS?

WAKE UP WITH A SNAKE IN YOUR
SLEEPING BAG OR A SPIDER ON
YOUR FACE?

5

LIVE WITHOUT YOUR BIG THUMB
OR ALL YOUR TOES?

6

SEE AN OPERA WITH YOUR
FRIENDS OR A ROCK CONCERT
WITH YOUR PARENTS?

7

GET SLAPPED BY A FRIEND OR
KISSED BY AN ENEMY?

8

9 BE BOILED ALIVE OR FROZEN TO DEATH?

10 GET BITTEN BY 100 MOSQUITOES OR STUNG BY 10 BEES?

11 GO TO CHURCH EVERY DAY FOR A WEEK OR NOT GO FOR A MONTH?

12 COACH YOUR FAVORITE SPORT OR REFEREE IT?

LIVE AS JOHN THE BAPTIST OR
THE APOSTLE PAUL? 13

SPEND A DAY ON A SUNNY
BEACH OR A SNOW COVERED
MOUNTAIN? 14

HAVE BODY ODOR OR BODY HAIR?
15

HAVE A REALLY BAD DATE WITH 16
SOMEONE YOU LIKE OR HAVE A
GREAT DATE WITH SOMEONE YOU
DON'T?

17 BE AN INCREDIBLE WRITER OR INCREDIBLE SPEAKER?

18 CHANGE YOUR FACE OR CHANGE YOUR BODY?

19 BE A ONE-HIT WONDER OR HAVE A LONG-BUT-MEDIOCRE MUSIC CAREER?

20 HAVE UNCONTROLLABLE BACK HAIR OR A FACE FULL OF WARTS?

**HAVE A HUGE NOSE OR
ENORMOUS EARS?**

21

**BE HATED FOR SOMETHING YOU
ARE OR LOVED FOR SOMETHING
YOU'RE NOT?**

22

**BREAK UP WITH SOMEONE OR BE
BROKEN UP WITH?**

23

**BE BALD FOR FIVE YEARS OR
HAVE A MULLET FOR LIFE?**

24

QUESTION 25

BE LOCKED IN A MENTAL
INSTITUTION WITH
PATIENTS OR STUCK IN
AN ELEVATOR FULL OF
THERAPISTS?

LIVE DURING JESUS' TIME OR BE
ALIVE WHEN JESUS RETURNS?

26

HAVE AN ARRANGED MARRIAGE
OR NEVER MARRY AT ALL?

27

BE AN EXTRA IN A BUNCH OF
MOVIES OR GET A MAJOR PART
IN ONE MOVIE?

28

29

BE LIED TO OR ABOUT?

HATE YOUR JOB AND
MAKE LOTS OF MONEY
OR LOVE YOUR JOB
AND BE POORLY PAID?

31

LICK FEET OR SNIFF SOMEONE'S ARMPIT?

32

ALLOW OTHERS TO SEE EVERYTHING YOU DO FOR A DAY OR HEAR EVERYTHING YOU SAY FOR A DAY?

33

WIN ON A CHEATING TEAM OR LOSE ON AN HONEST TEAM?

34 DIE BRAVELY FROM A TERRIBLE DISEASE WHILE INSPIRING OTHERS OR LIVE IN GREAT HEALTH ALL YOUR LIFE AND NEVER MAKE A DIFFERENCE IN THE WORLD?

35 SPEND THE DAY AT THE BEACH OR ON A SNOW-CAPPED MOUNTAIN?

36 BE AN IDENTICAL TWIN OR AN ONLY CHILD?

37 BREAK UP A FIGHT OR WATCH ONE?

WRITE A BOOK OR BE THE
OBJECT OF ONE?

38

FIND A HAIR IN YOUR LAST BITE
OF HAMBURGER OR A BUG IN
THE BOTTOM OF YOUR DRINK?

39

HAVE YOUR PARENTS SAY "I LOVE
YOU" OR "YOU'RE RIGHT"?

40

FIGHT IN A CURRENT-DAY WAR
OR A MIDDLE-AGES WAR WITHOUT
THE ADVANCED MACHINERY?

41

42 SKYDIVE OR BUNGEE JUMP?

43 HAVE A SCAR STORY INVOLVING AN ALLIGATOR OR A SHARK?

44 BE GLUED TO AN AIRPLANE OR A CRUISE SHIP?

45 RIDE A ROLLER COASTER OR A WATER SLIDE?

46 HAVE AN APPOINTMENT WITH A PROCTOLOGIST FOR AN HOUR OR BE ONE FOR A DAY?

47

CRUSADE TO SAVE THE WHALES
OR THE TREES?

48

BE RICH AND SINGLE OR POOR
AND HAPPILY MARRIED?

49

WATCH AN EXECUTION OR A BABY
BEING DELIVERED?

50

DONATE MONEY TO AN
ORPHANAGE OR VOLUNTEER AT
A NURSING HOME?

GO WITHOUT SLEEP FOR A WEEK
OR WITHOUT A SHOWER FOR A
MONTH?

51

DATE A GORGEOUS PERSON WITH
CHRONIC BAD BREATH OR AN
AVERAGE LOOKING PERSON WITH
MINTY-FRESH BREATH?

52

SPEND YOUR LIFE IN A U.S.
PRISON (WITHOUT PAROLE) OR
AS A HOSTAGE IN A FOREIGN
COUNTRY (IN A PALACE)?

53

54 DOGSLED ACROSS ALASKA OR RIVER RAFT ACROSS COLORADO?

55 ENDURE A STRAITJACKET FOR A WEEK OR HANDCUFFS FOR A MONTH?

56 BE LOST FOR 10 MINUTES AND ASK FOR DIRECTIONS OR BE LOST FOR 2 HOURS AND FIND THE DESTINATION ON YOUR OWN?

57 HAVE A REPUTATION AS A GOSSIP OR A LIAR?

GET AN A ON A TEST BECAUSE YOU STUDIED FOR WEEKS OR GET A C WITHOUT STUDYING AT ALL?

58

HAVE A COMPUTER OR A CELL PHONE?

59

PASS ON GOOD VALUES TO YOUR CHILDREN OR A LARGE INHERITANCE?

60

61

HAVE FIGHTING PARENTS WHO STAY TOGETHER OR PARENTS WHO GET DIVORCED?

62 RENT A MOVIE AND WATCH IT AT HOME OR PAY FOR A TICKET AND WATCH IT AT THE THEATER?

63 HAVE UNLIMITED ACCESS TO THE INTERNET OR TELEVISION?

64 BE ABLE TO ALWAYS REMEMBER OR BE ABLE TO ALWAYS FORGET?

65 BE ATTRACTIVE AND DIE YOUNG OR BE UGLY AND DIE OLD?

66 SPEND A WHOLE DAY WATCHING YOUR FAVORITE MOVIES OR EATING YOUR FAVORITE FOODS?

67 LIVE IN A SHACK ON THE BEACH OR A SMALL CABIN IN THE MOUNTAINS?

68 WORK HARD FIRST THEN PLAY LATER OR PLAY FIRST THEN WORK HARD LATER?

69 HAVE THE STRENGTH OF GOLIATH OR THE ACCURACY OF DAVID?

BE INVISIBLE OR HAVE X-RAY VISION? 70

NEVER BRUSH YOUR TEETH OR NEVER WASH YOUR BODY? 71

HAVE A PERFECT MARRIAGE FOR TWO YEARS THAT ENDS IN TRAGEDY OR HAVE A BAD MARRIAGE FOR 25 YEARS? 72

TAKE A BATH WITH A HUNGRY SNAKE OR A SCARED CAT? 73

CATCH YOUR OWN FOOD OR GROW YOUR OWN FOOD?

74

WATCH THE WEATHER CHANNEL ON A BIG-SCREEN TV ALL DAY OR WATCH THE SUPER BOWL ON A TWO-INCH BLACK AND WHITE WITH NO SOUND?

75

LEARN SIGN LANGUAGE OR LEARN TO READ BRAILLE?

76

PASS GAS LOUDLY IN CHURCH OR ON A FIRST DATE?

77

BE A SINGER OR A COMEDIAN?

78

MISTAKE A WOMAN FOR BEING PREGNANT OR FOR BEING A MAN?

79

BATHE YOUR GRANDPARENTS EVERY DAY OR BE BATHED BY YOUR GRANDPARENTS EVERY DAY?

80

WATCH A ROMANTIC MOVIE SCENE WITH YOUR PARENTS OR ONE INVOLVING YOUR PARENTS?

81

MORE WOULD YOU RATHER

37

THROW UP FOR A WHOLE WEEK OR NOT EAT FOR A WHOLE WEEK?

82

LINE DANCE OR BALLROOM DANCE?

83

HAVE YOUR WISDOM TEETH PULLED OR GET 25 STITCHES ACROSS YOUR CHIN?

84

TAKE A PILL AND BE SICK FOR A WEEK OR GET 7 SHOTS AND BE SICK FOR 1 DAY?

85

**BE THE
QUARTERBACK
OR THE
PITCHER?**

87

BE LOST IN A CAVE OR IN A DESERT?

88

EAT A BOWL OF JALAPEÑOS OR A BOWL OF PRUNES?

89

SMELL LIKE AN ARMPIT OR LIKE DIRTY SOCKS?

90

HEAR THE SONG "HAPPY BIRTHDAY" IN YOUR HEAD FOR ETERNITY OR NEVER HEAR MUSIC AGAIN?

91 BE ABDUCTED BY ALIENS OR STARVING CANNIBALS?

92 BE A MISSIONARY TO AFRICA OR CHINA?

93 HAVE ALL YOUR TV CHANNELS PERMANENTLY SHOW INFOMERCIALS OR TV EVANGELISTS?

94 BE A HIP-HOP STAR OR A POP STAR?

GET BEATEN UP BY A MOM OR A NUN? 95

RESOLVE A CONFLICT WITH A FRIEND OVER THE PHONE OR VIA E-MAIL? 96

EAT ROTTEN EGGS OR ROTTEN MEAT? 97

BE ADDICTED TO VIDEO GAMES OR TV? 98

99 BE ADDICTED TO GAMBLING OR DRUGS?

100 GET A TATTOO OR NOSE RING?

101 HEAL A LEPER OR TURN WATER INTO WINE?

102 BE LOVING OR ALWAYS RIGHT?

GET HIT WITH A BASEBALL BAT OR KICKED BY A HORSE? 103

READ A LONG, INTRIGUING MYSTERY OR A SHORT, DULL COMIC BOOK? 104

BE A SHOOTER ON THE FIRING SQUAD OR THE ONE GIVING THE ORDER TO FIRE? 105

CLAIM CHRIST AND BE PUT TO DEATH OR DENY CHRIST TO SPARE THE LIVES OF OTHERS? 106

107 START A FIRE OR PUT ONE OUT?

108 GET THE ELECTRIC CHAIR OR THE GAS CHAMBER?

109 BE A SOLDIER IN THE AMERICAN REVOLUTION OR THE CIVIL WAR?

110 GO TO SUMMER SCHOOL OR TRAFFIC SCHOOL?

PRAY FOR AN HOUR OR READ THE BIBLE FOR AN HOUR?

111

GET MARRIED AND HAVE YOUR SPOUSE CHEAT ON YOU OR NEVER GET MARRIED AT ALL?

112

113

SKATEBOARD OR IN-LINE SKATE?

BE NAMED AFTER A FRUIT OR VEGETABLE?

114

1   1   5

HAVE SOMEONE POINT OUT A BOOGER STUCK TO THE EDGE OF YOUR NOSTRIL OR A PIECE OF TOILET PAPER HANGING OUTSIDE YOUR PANTS?

116

HAVE AN INDOOR JOB OR AN OUTSIDE JOB?

EAT A DOG OR EAT A CAT?

BE A COWBOY OR A PIRATE?

BE A HEAVYWEIGHT BOXER OR A RACECAR DRIVER?

120 DIE A FAST, PAINFUL DEATH OR
LIVE A LONG, BORING LIFE?

121 HAVE NO EYEBROWS OR NO
FINGERNAILS?

122 HAVE FOUR TINY EYES OR ONE
MASSIVE EYE?

123 BE COVERED WITH FUR OR
COVERED WITH SCALES?

LOSE THE ABILITY TO TASTE OR THE ABILITY TO SMELL?

124

FILE YOUR TEETH DOWN TO THE GUMS OR HAVE YOUR TOES CHOPPED OFF?

125

SLEEP FOR ONE NIGHT IN AN ITCHING-POWDER BED OR WEAR A POISON IVY SUIT FOR A WEEK?

126

HAVE A FOOT-LONG NOSE OR A FOOT-LONG TONGUE?

127

YOUR MOM DIDN'T SHAVE HER LEGS OR YOUR DAD SHAVED HIS?

128

TALK LIKE YODA OR BREATHE LIKE DARTH VADER?

129

HEAR JESUS DELIVER A SERMON OR WRITE ONE FOR HIM?

130

SNOW SKI IN YOUR SWIMSUIT OR WATER-SKI IN YOUR SNOWSUIT?

131

ENDURE 40 PERCENT OF YOUR BODY COVERED IN SCABS OR 10 PERCENT COVERED WITH MOLES?

BRING ABOUT LASTING WORLD
PEACE OR ELIMINATE ALL
HUNGER AND DISEASE?

133

LAUGH OR MAKE OTHERS
LAUGH?

134

HAVE YOUR ENTIRE COMMUNITY
FACE A TORNADO OR A
TERRORIST ATTACK?

135

BE A PHOTOGRAPHER OR A PAINTER?

1,36

SEE IN COLOR OR HAVE NIGHT VISION?

137

GO THREE ROUNDS WITH SAMPSON OR GOLIATH?

1,38

LIVE LIFE IN OZ (AS IN THE WIZARD OF OZ) OR IN WONDERLAND (ALICE IN WONDERLAND)?

139

140 HAVE OUT-OF-CONTROL CURLY HAIR OR STRAIGHT HAIR YOU COULD NEVER CHANGE?

141 HAVE A NOTICEABLE OVERBITE OR UNDERBITE?

142 ORGANIZE A WINNING PRESIDENTIAL CAMPAIGN OR BE THE CANDIDATE FOR THE LOSING PARTY?

143 JAM YOUR FINGER OR STUB YOUR TOE?

144
TALK LIKE DAFFY DUCK OR ELMER FUDD?

145
GET STRANDED ON AN ISLAND WITHOUT FIRE OR WITHOUT A FRIEND?

146
OWN A SAILBOAT OR A SPEEDBOAT?

147
HAVE HORNS ON YOUR HEAD OR A FOUR-FOOT TAIL?

148 TREAT OTHERS WITH KINDNESS
OR ALWAYS BE TREATED WITH
KINDNESS?

GET LOCKED OUT OF YOUR
HOUSE NAKED OR TRIP AND
FALL ON YOUR WEDDING DAY?

149

BUILD HOMES YOU COULD NEVER
AFFORD OR MAKE CLOTHES YOU
COULD NEVER WEAR?

150

GET A SPEEDING TICKET OR
HAVE A MINOR WRECK?

151

152 SEE INTO YOUR FUTURE OR CHANGE YOUR PAST?

153 GET DUMPED OVER THE PHONE OR BY E-MAIL?

154 ENTERTAIN ON STAGE OR SERVE BACKSTAGE?

155 INTERVIEW GOD OR INTERVIEW SATAN?

156 DISCOVER THAT YOUR SPOUSE HAD A SEX CHANGE OR WAS A SERIAL KILLER?

157 FORGET THE ALPHABET OR HOW TO COUNT?

158 DATE THE PASTOR'S KID OR THE POLICE CHIEF'S KID?

159 LOSE YOUR SENSE OF TOUCH OR YOUR ABILITY TO EXPERIENCE EMOTIONS?

GET STUFFED IN A LOCKER OR
GET YOUR HEAD FLUSHED IN A
TOILET?
160

HEAR VOICES IN YOUR HEAD OR
NOTICE THAT EVERYONE YOU
MEET IS STARING AT YOU?
161

GO THREE DAYS WITHOUT FOOD
OR THREE DAYS WITHOUT
SLEEP?
162

ARGUE WHEN YOU KNOW YOU'RE
WRONG OR KEEP SILENT WHEN
YOU KNOW YOU'RE RIGHT?
163

164

BE THE CLASS CLOWN OR THE TEACHER'S PET?

165

NEVER HAVE SALT AGAIN OR NEVER HAVE SUGAR AGAIN?

166

GET COVERED WITH SLUGS OR COVERED WITH CRICKETS?

167

HAVE THREE WISHES YOU CAN USE FOR OTHERS OR ONE WISH YOU CAN KEEP FOR YOURSELF?

168 BE A RODEO CLOWN OR THE BULL?

169 SAY EVERYTHING YOU'RE THINKING OR NEVER SPEAK AGAIN?

170 PUBLISH YOUR DIARY OR MAKE A MOVIE ABOUT YOUR MOST EMBARRASSING MOMENTS?

171 FORGET WHO YOU ARE OR WHO EVERYONE ELSE IS?

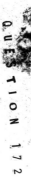

QUESTION 172

WRITE THE WORST
BOOK IN HISTORY
OR RECORD THE
WORST SONG?

173

EAT RAW FISH FOR DINNER
OR DRINK RAW EGGS FOR
BREAKFAST?

174

BE INTELLECTUALLY TALENTED
OR PHYSICALLY STRONG?

175

BE A CRIME-SCENE
INVESTIGATOR OR SEARCH FOR
KIDNAPPED CHILDREN?

176

READ THE OLD TESTAMENT OR
THE NEW TESTAMENT?

DISCOVER BIG FOOT OR THE
LOCH NESS MONSTER?

177

HAVE MULTIPLE PERSONALITIES
OR NO PERSONALITY AT ALL?

178

BE TORTURED BY TICKLING OR
BY WATER SLOWLY DRIPPING ON
YOUR FOREHEAD?

179

BE A JUNIOR HIGH CAMP
COUNSELOR OR GET EATEN BY A
PACK OF HUNGRY WOLVES?

180

181 BE IN A CHRISTIAN BAND THAT HELPS BELIEVERS OR A SECULAR BAND THAT INSPIRES NON-BELIEVERS?

182 TAKE A GREEK ISLAND CRUISE OR HIKE THE HIMALAYAS?

183 DRINK A GLASS OF VINEGAR OR A GLASS OF SOY SAUCE?

184 HAVE CHRONIC BACK PAIN OR RECURRING MIGRAINES?

BITE YOUR TONGUE OR STUB YOUR TOE?

185

BE UNABLE TO LAUGH AGAIN OR UNABLE TO CRY AGAIN?

186

ALWAYS EAT FROM DIRTY DISHES OR ALWAYS WEAR DIRTY CLOTHES?

187

GET STUCK AT THE TOP OF A FERRIS WHEEL FOR 24 HOURS OR ON A NONSTOP ROLLER COASTER FOR EIGHT HOURS?

188

189 GET STUCK IN A FLATULENCE-FILLED ELEVATOR OR IN A KIDDIE POOL FILLED WITH URINE?

190 GET A COLLEGE SCHOLARSHIP OR A RECORDING CONTRACT?

191 BE RIDICULED FOR A DAY OR IGNORED FOR A WEEK?

192 WALK A TIGHT ROPE OVER A POOL OF PIRANHAS OR WALK THROUGH A 10-MILE TUNNEL IN COMPLETE DARKNESS?

LIVE WITH A MURDERER OR BE ONE?

193

LIVE ONLY BY NIGHT OR ONLY BY DAY?

194

HAVE HEAD LICE OR ATHLETE'S FOOT?

195

SLEEP IN A ROOM FULL OF HORNETS THAT MIGHT STING OR A ROOM FULL OF MOSQUITOES THAT WILL BITE?

196

HAVE NO SENSE OF BALANCE
OR NO SENSE OF HUMOR? 197

BE CONSIDERED MEAN OR
GULLIBLE? 198

HAVE ONLY ONE BOOK TO READ
OR ONE CD TO LISTEN TO? 199

LIVE 2,000 YEARS IN THE
FUTURE OR 2,000 YEARS IN THE
PAST? 200

DESTROY EVERYTHING YOU HAVE EVER CREATED OR NEVER BE ABLE TO CREATE AGAIN?

201

HAVE A LISP OR A STUTTER?

202

HAVE NO FRIENDS OR ENEMIES OR HAVE MANY OF BOTH?

203

BE CONSTANTLY MISUNDERSTOOD OR NEVER ABLE TO UNDERSTAND ANYBODY?

204

HAVE A FAILING MEMORY OR
FAILING EYESIGHT?

SPEND A YEAR WITH ONLY MEN
OR ONLY WOMEN? 206

FIND TRUE LOVE OR A MILLION
DOLLARS? 207

TRAVEL WITH JESUS FOR
THREE YEARS OR HELP START
CHURCHES WITH THE APOSTLE
PAUL FOR 10 YEARS? 208

BE KNOWN FOR YOUR
REPUTATION OR FOR YOUR
LOOKS? 209

BE ABLE TO FAST FORWARD
LIFE OR REWIND IT?
210

BE THE GODFATHER OF SOUL OR
THE KING OF ROCK 'N' ROLL?
211

BE CALLED TO MISSION IN A
FAR OFF LAND OR TO BE A
MISSIONARY IN THE INNER CITY?
212

HAVE A RECURRING NIGHTMARE
THAT YOU'RE FALLING OR THAT
YOU'RE NAKED IN PUBLIC?
213

**HAVE YOUR WEIGHT CHANGE
EVERY DAY OR YOUR HEIGHT
CHANGE EVERY DAY?**

2   1,   4

**TEACH ENGLISH IN A FOREIGN
COUNTRY OR TEACH A FOREIGN
LANGUAGE TO AMERICANS?**

2   1,   5

**MAKE BAD DECISIONS OR BE
INDECISIVE?**

2   1,

6

**EVERYONE KNOW YOU'RE A
CHRISTIAN AND HATE YOU OR
SUSPECT YOU'RE AN ATHEIST
AND LOVE YOU?**

2   1,   7

SLEEP IN THE RAIN OR IN A
SANDSTORM?

218

LIVE IN AN ORGANIZED HOME
AND NOT BE ABLE TO FIND A
THING OR LIVE IN A PIGSTY AND
KNOW WHERE EVERYTHING IS?

219

HAVE YOUR LITTLE BROTHER
OR SISTER TAG ALONG ON YOUR
DREAM DATE OR SHADOW YOU AT
SCHOOL FOR A MONTH?

220

BE RIGHT MORALLY BUT WRONG
LEGALLY OR BE RIGHT LEGALLY
BUT WRONG MORALLY?

221

OWN AN AWESOME SPORTS CAR OR AN AWESOME TRUCK? **222**

LEAD SINGING AT YOUR CHURCH OR PREACH THE MESSAGE? **223**

WORK FOR SOMEONE ELSE AND BE UNDERPAID BUT HAVE JOB SECURITY OR START YOUR OWN COMPANY WITH NO GUARANTEED INCOME BUT HAVE THE CHANCE TO MAKE MILLIONS? **224**

225 SPEND AN HOUR LOOKING FOR THE REMOTE CONTROL OR GET UP ALL DAY TO CHANGE THE CHANNEL?

226 SLEEP ON THE TOP BUNK OR THE BOTTOM BUNK?

227 WET YOUR PANTS EVERY TIME YOU LAUGH OR NEVER GET ANYBODY'S JOKES?

228 WORK FOR THE CIA OR AS PART OF A S.W.A.T. TEAM?

229 CAUSE AN ACCIDENT THAT LEAVES A STRANGER DEAD OR A FRIEND CRIPPLED FOR LIFE?

230 AGE ONLY FROM THE NECK UP OR AGE ONLY FROM THE NECK DOWN?

231 WALK ON WATER FOREVER OR FLY FOR A WEEK?

232 BE A LAWYER OR A JUDGE?

HELP CHANGE PEOPLE'S MINDS OR PEOPLE'S HEARTS?

233

BE A MECHANIC AND OWN YOUR OWN GARAGE OR WORK AT THE WHITE HOUSE IN A LOW-LEVEL JOB?

234

CONSISTENTLY ARRIVE 30 MINUTES LATE OR 60 MINUTES EARLY?

235

GET WOKEN UP BY A DRUM LINE OR BY COLD WATER THROWN IN YOUR FACE?

236

BE EFFICIENT OR EFFECTIVE?
237

**OWN A HIGH-RISE PENTHOUSE OR
A SOUTHERN MANSION?**
238

**LIVE ON WELFARE OR ALWAYS
ASK YOUR FAMILY FOR MONEY?**
239

**SHARE YOUR FAITH STORY
BEFORE A CROWD OF CHRISTIANS
OR NON-CHRISTIANS?**
240

241. FALL DOWN EVERY FLIGHT OF STAIRS YOU STEP ON OR NEVER RUN?

242 BREAK THE LAND SPEED RECORD OR THE AIR SPEED RECORD?

243 LIVE EVERY MINUTE OF YOUR LIFE ON CAMERA OR NEVER BE NOTICED BY ANYONE?

244 HAVE A STALKER OR BE A STALKER?

HAVE COURTSIDE SEATS TO AN NBA GAME OR NFL SEATS ON THE 50-YARD LINE?

245

HAVE A NAME EVERYBODY MAKES FUN OF OR ONE THAT'S DIFFICULT TO PRONOUNCE?

246

HAVE PERFECT PITCH OR PERFECT RHYTHM?

247

BE BORN A CONJOINED TWIN OR WITHOUT ARMS?

248

249 KNOW HOW TO CHANGE A CAR'S OIL OR HOW TO CHANGE A FLAT TIRE?

250 COMMUNICATE ONLY IN PIG LATIN OR ONLY IN SIGN LANGUAGE?

251 HAVE YOUR DOCTOR GIVE YOU A SHOT RIGHT NEXT TO YOUR EYE OR 20 SHOTS IN YOUR BELLY BUTTON?

252 HAVE A SEVERE STUTTER OR SING EVERY WORD YOU SPEAK?

HAVE A PAPER CUT ON YOUR
TONGUE OR BETWEEN YOUR
INDEX AND MIDDLE FINGERS?

254

FIGHT A WAR FOR FREEDOM OR FOR EQUALITY?

255

GIVE UP YOUR FREEDOM OF SPEECH OR YOUR RIGHT TO VOTE?

256

SPRAIN YOUR ANKLE OR JAM YOUR WRIST?

257

READ SOMEONE'S MIND OR UNDERSTAND SOMEONE'S HEART?

MEET YOUR FAVORITE ATHLETE
OR YOUR FAVORITE ACTOR?

 258

MEET YOUR FAVORITE MUSICIAN
OR YOUR FAVORITE AUTHOR? 259

LEAD SOMEONE TO JESUS OR
LIVE LIKE JESUS?

260

WALK BACKWARD TO GET
WHERE YOU'RE GOING OR DO 261
CARTWHEELS TO GET THERE?

262 LOOK GOOD OR FEEL GOOD?

263 BEGIN LIVING THE "CHRISTIAN LIFE" IN YOUR TEENS OR LIVE A "PARTY LIFE" AND TURN TO GOD IN YOUR 90s?

264 WITNESS A MURDER OR SOLVE ONE?

265 BE CLUELESS OR CARELESS?

LISTEN TO BABIES CRY OR YOUR FRIENDS WHINE?

266

HAVE DISCOVERED FIRE OR ELECTRICITY?

267

BE EMBARRASSED OR FRUSTRATED?

268

HAVE PARENTS THAT ARE TOO STRICT OR TOO PERMISSIVE?

269

HAVE FALSE TEETH OR A GLASS EYE?

270

RUN A MARATHON OR SWIM 10 MILES?

271

FEEL GUILT OR PHYSICAL PAIN?

272

DRINK FROM THE FOUNTAIN OF YOUTH OR REST IN THE GARDEN OF EDEN?

273

WORK IN THE FAMILY BUSINESS OR BE THE FIRST ONE FROM YOUR FAMILY TO WORK IN A PARTICULAR FIELD?

FALL OUT OF A MOVING CAR OR BE TRAMPLED BY AN ANGRY HORSE?

275

BE ABLE TO FLY OR ABLE TO WALK THROUGH WALLS?

6

7

2

INVENT SOMETHING AMAZING AND NEVER RECEIVE CREDIT OR BECOME RICH, FAMOUS, AND INFLUENTIAL AFTER STEALING SOMEONE ELSE'S IDEA?

2   7   7

DIG FOR MUMMIES OR DIVE FOR SPANISH GOLD?

278

GET CAPTURED BY HITLER OR ATTILA THE HUN?

279

WRITE A SPORTS COLUMN OR AN ADVICE COLUMN?

280

TAKE COMMUNION OR LEAD OTHERS TO TAKE COMMUNION?

281

HAVE A HIGH IQ OR COMMON SENSE?

282

283
LIVE IN A HAUNTED HOUSE OR A FUN HOUSE?

284
WORK AT A CARNIVAL OR A ZOO?

285
START A MINISTRY OR SERVE IN ONE?

286
BE A NOTORIOUS OUTLAW OR A NOTORIOUS POLITICIAN?

BE A MORTICIAN OR A TAXIDERMIST?

287

STOMP GRAPES OR POP BUBBLE WRAP?

288

HAVE AN ITCH THAT YOU CAN'T SCRATCH OR HICCUPS THAT WON'T GO AWAY?

289

COME IN LAST PLACE AT THE OLYMPICS OR FIRST PLACE AT YOUR SCHOOL'S STATE CHAMPIONSHIP?

290

BE FORGETFUL OR
THOUGHTLESS? 291

BE OVERWEIGHT OR
UNDERNOURISHED?
292

BAG GROCERIES OR WORK AT A
FAST-FOOD RESTAURANT? 293

LEGALIZE MARIJUANA OR ALL
FORMS OF PORNOGRAPHY? 294

295 BAN ALCOHOL OR SMOKING?

CLEAN YOUR ROOM OR MOW THE LAWN?

296

RUN FAST OR THINK QUICKLY ON YOUR FEET?

297

EARN A MILLION DOLLARS OR WIN A MILLION DOLLARS?

298

299 LIVE ON THE EAST COAST OR THE WEST COAST?

300 ATTEND THE OSCARS OR THE GRAMMIES?

301 SING THE NATIONAL ANTHEM AT THE WORLD SERIES OR BE THE HALFTIME ENTERTAINMENT FOR THE SUPER BOWL?

302 WORK IN A CHILDREN'S CANCER CENTER OR IN A NURSING HOME?

CHANGE A BEDPAN OR CLEAN UP VOMIT?

303

DISCOVER YOU WERE ADOPTED OR THAT YOUR DAD ISN'T YOUR BIOLOGICAL FATHER?

304

RIDE A RAGING BULL OR BE A BULLFIGHTER?

305

TOUR WORLD FAMOUS MUSEUMS OR BATTLEFIELDS?

306

307

TOUR CELEBRITY HOMES OR
NOTORIOUS CRIME SCENES?

308

PUSH AN OLD LADY DOWN OR
TRIP A TODDLER?

309

TEACH LIKE JESUS OR LIVE LIKE
JESUS?

310

BITE YOUR OWN TOENAILS OR
SOMEONE ELSE'S FINGERNAILS?

BE IN LOVE ONCE OR
INFATUATED DAILY?

311

WITNESS THE PARTING OF THE
RED SEA OR JESUS WALKING ON
WATER?

312

WRITE A CHILDREN'S BOOK OR
CREATE A HIT JINGLE FOR A TV
COMMERCIAL?

313

BE A GARBAGE COLLECTOR OR A
CHIMNEY SWEEP?

314

BE THE LIFE OF THE PARTY WITH NO TRUE FRIENDSHIPS OR A TOTAL WALLFLOWER WITH ONE AMAZING BEST FRIEND? 315

TAKE A BULLET TO THE CHEST OR A KNIFE TO THE BACK? 316

CONTROL OTHERS OR YOUR FUTURE? 317

STOP TIME OR FAST-FORWARD IT? 318

319 WRITE A BEST-SELLING BOOK OR BE IN A HALL OF FAME?

320 WEAR PLATFORM SHOES OR SIX-INCH, STILETTO HEELS?

321 BE A MEMBER OF THE ROLLING STONES OR A MEMBER OF THE BEATLES?

322 HOST A RADIO SHOW OR TV SHOW?

323

POSE NUDE FOR AN ART CLASS OF 10 OR SPEAK IN PUBLIC TO A CROWD OF 10,000?

TRAVEL THE WORLD OR BE A MISSIONARY?

324

BE WISE OR BE LUCKY?

325

HICCUP FOR A WEEK OR SNEEZE FOR A WEEK?

326

ANSWER THE PHONE AND BE HUNG UP ON OR ANSWER THE DOOR AND HAVE NO ONE BE THERE?

327

328 HAVE YOUR EYES SEWN SHUT OR YOUR MOUTH?

329 PREACH TO THOUSANDS AT A CRUSADE OR GO DOOR-TO-DOOR AND TALK ABOUT JESUS?

330 EAT POPSICLES EVERY DAY OR BROWNIES EVERY DAY?

331 FEED YOUR MIND OR YOUR BODY?

BE AN HISTORIAN OR A
COMPUTER PROGRAMMER?

333 BE MIGHTY MOUSE OR MICKEY MOUSE?

334 BE DAFFY DUCK OR DONALD DUCK?

335 BE AN ELECTRICIAN OR A PLUMBER?

TRAVEL THE WORLD ON A WHIRLWIND TOUR OR SPEND A MONTH IN JUST ONE COUNTRY SOAKING UP THE CULTURE?

336

BITE INTO AN EGGSHELL WHILE EATING AN OMELET OR A BONE WHILE EATING A CHICKEN SANDWICH?

337

HAVE NO KNEES OR NO ELBOWS?

338

GET SLAPPED IN THE FACE OR PUNCHED IN THE GUT?

339

GET ADVICE FROM A FORTUNE TELLER OR A DREAM ANALYST?

340

EAT PIE OR CAKE?

341

DRINK APPLE JUICE OR ORANGE JUICE?

342

DRIVE A BUS OR AN 18-WHEELER?

343

COMMAND AN AIRCRAFT CARRIER OR A SUBMARINE?

344

BE THE SUPERHERO OR THE SUPERHERO'S SIDEKICK?

345

DONATE A KIDNEY OR A LUNG?

346

BE THE FASTEST TALKER IN THE WORLD OR THE FASTEST READER IN THE WORLD?

347

348

POSSESS THE
ABILITY TO
SPEED READ
OR MEMORIZE
EVERYTHING YOU
READ?

STAPLE GUN YOUR FINGER OR
SHOOT A NAIL GUN THROUGH
YOUR TOE?

349

BE CLAUSTROPHOBIC
(FEAR OF SMALL SPACES) OR
AGORAPHOBIC (FEAR OF OPEN
SPACES)?

350

BE THE PRESIDENT OF THE
UNITED STATES OR THE
PRESIDENT OF A FAMOUS
SPORTS' FRANCHISE?

351

BE A MARINE BIOLOGIST OR A ZOOKEEPER?

PLUCK A CHICKEN OR SHEAR A LAMB? 353

EAT PIG'S FEET OR COW TONGUE? 354

EAT MONKEY BRAIN OR ROCKY MOUNTAIN OYSTERS? 355

LEAD A REVOLUTION OR A PEACE DEMONSTRATION? 356

READ THE BOOK OF MORMON OR THE KORAN? 357

LIVE IN A COMMUNIST COUNTRY OR A SOCIALIST COUNTRY? 358

YOUR NOSE GREW WHEN YOU LIED OR TURNED BRIGHT RED WHEN YOU'RE ATTRACTED TO SOMEONE? 359

360

BE INCREDIBLY ORGANIZED OR INCREDIBLY CREATIVE?

BEG OR STEAL?

361

PLAY THE GUITAR OR THE DRUMS?

362

BE THE LEAD SINGER OR A RUNWAY MODEL?

363

BE A BIRD WATCHER OR A BUTTERFLY ENTHUSIAST?

364

365 GO TO A CHURCH CAMP OR A SPORTS CAMP?

BE A MOVIE CRITIC OR A MUSIC CRITIC?

366

FIGURE SKATE OR FINGER PAINT?

367

BE A TIGHTROPE WALKER OR A TRAPEZE ARTIST?

368

369

**SHARE YOUR FAITH IN A
HOMELESS SHELTER OR
WORK WITHOUT TALKING?**

STARE AT THE SUN OR LIE IN A
SCORPION BED?

370

DRIVE MONSTER TRUCKS OR BE
A PROFESSIONAL WRESTLER?

371

DREAM ABOUT BEING CHASED
BY MEAN PUPPETS OR SCARY
CLOWNS?

372

373 WATCH AN OPERA OR THE BALLET?

374 SCULPT CLAY WITH A SEWING NEEDLE OR CREATE A PORTRAIT WITH A PAINTBALL GUN?

375 WATCH A FUNNY MOVIE OR A SCARY ONE?

376 HAVE A WOODPECKER TAPPING AT YOUR SKULL OR PIRANHAS NIPPING AT YOUR TOES?

BE EMBARRASSED OR ANGRY? 377

THE WORLD BELIEVED ONE RELIGION OR HAD FREEDOM OF RELIGION UNDER ONE WORLD GOVERNMENT? 378

HAVE PARENTS WHO MAKE YOU FEEL GUILTY OR WHO NAG? 379

BE A DEBT COLLECTOR OR A BOUNTY HUNTER? 380

381

PROTEST
SANTA
CLAUS OR
THE EASTER
BUNNY?

WRECK YOUR MOM'S CAR OR YOUR DAD'S CAR?

382

BE A SKATEBOARDER OR A SNOWBOARDER?

383

SELL POPCORN UP AND DOWN THE STEPS OF A SPORTS STADIUM OR DRESS UP IN A GORILLA COSTUME AND WAVE AT PEOPLE IN FRONT OF A MOVIE THEATRE?

384

SLOWLY COME TO KNOW CHRIST OR HAVE A "ROAD TO DAMASCUS" EXPERIENCE?

385

SHARE YOUR FAITH WITH JEWS OR MUSLIMS?

386

BE THE FIRST MAN/WOMAN ON EARTH OR THE LAST MAN/WOMAN ON EARTH?

387

BE AN ACTION FIGURE OR A PIN-UP POSTER?

388

389 BE LOCKED IN SOLITARY CONFINEMENT OR IMPRISONED AS A P.O.W.?

390 BE A SUNDAY SCHOOL VOLUNTEER OR WORK THE INFO BOOTH AT DISNEYLAND?

391 RACE CARS OR SPEEDBOATS?

392 GO ON A DATE WITH THE SCHOOL PSYCHO OR WITH THE SCHOOL HOTTIE, CHAPERONED BY YOUR PARENT?

BE A CHILDHOOD FRIEND OF YOUR PARENTS OR KNOW EXACTLY WHAT THEY DID WHEN THEY WERE IN COLLEGE?

BE THE SMARTEST, MOST CREATIVE PERSON IN THE WORLD OR KNOW HOW TO GET THE SMARTEST, MOST CREATIVE PERSON IN THE WORLD TO WORK FOR YOU?

394

SCREAM AT THE TOP OF YOUR LUNGS FOR AN HOUR OR HAVE YOUR EYES FORCED SHUT FOR A DAY?

395

HAVE SWEATY HANDS OR SWEATY FEET?

396

HAVE A FIVE-MINUTE ATTENTION
SPAN OR BE NARCOLEPTIC
(FALL INTO A SUDDEN DEEP
SLEEP WITHOUT WARNING)? 397

EAT THAI FOOD OR INDIAN FOOD? 398

BE A BELLY DANCER OR A MIME? 399

MAKE CHILDREN LAUGH OR OLD
PEOPLE CRY? 400

401
TAKE RISKS WITH YOUR LIFE OR
RISKS WITH YOUR MONEY?

402
BE A COMPULSIVE LIAR OR A
KLEPTOMANIAC?

403
DESIGN WEB SITES OR
BILLBOARDS?

404
HAVE THE ABILITY TO TELEPORT
TO OTHER PLACES OR MOVE
OBJECTS WITH YOUR MIND?

STUDY DECOMPOSING BODIES OR
MUTATIONS IN AMPHIBIANS? 4 0 5

BE AN AIR TRAFFIC CONTROLLER
OR A METEOROLOGIST? 4 0 6

BE A DARTS CHAMPION OR A
BILLIARDS CHAMPION? 4 0 7

408

LIVE WITH YOUR PARENTS UNTIL YOU TURN 30 OR HAVE YOUR PARENTS LIVE WITH YOU AFTER YOU TURN 50?

BLEED MAPLE SYRUP OR
SNEEZE GRAPE JELLY?
409

DRINK SPRITE OR 7-UP?
410

FLY IN A HOT-AIR BALLOON OR A
BLIMP?
411

HAVE A FACE THAT COULD STOP
A CLOCK (UGLY) OR A LAUGH
THAT COULD WAKE THE DEAD
(OBNOXIOUS)?
412

BE A KNOW-IT-ALL OR A TELL-IT-ALL? 413

413

413

PET A PORCUPINE OR LICK A CACTUS? 414

414

414

BE THE WORLD CHAMPION AT CHESS OR SCRABBLE? 415

415

415

BE TOLD YOU'RE BORING OR TOLD YOU'RE STUPID? 416

416

416

417

HIBERNATE FOR THE WINTER OR
HIBERNATE FOR THE SUMMER?

418

HAVE THE DISCIPLINE OF A MARTIAL ARTIST OR THE CREATIVITY OF A PAINTER?

419

HAVE A BLOCKHEAD OR A BUBBLE BUTT?

420

WORK ON A DEMOLITION CREW OR BUILD HOUSES?

421 RAKE LEAVES OR SHOVEL SNOW?

422 HAVE YOUR HAIR FALL OUT OR YOUR TEETH FALL OUT?

423 BE A MIDDLE CHILD OR AN ONLY CHILD?

424 BE A YOUTH PASTOR OR A SENIOR PASTOR?

WOULD YOU RATHER... THE WORLD SPOKE ONE LANGUAGE OR USED THE SAME CURRENCY?

BE IN BAND OR IN CHOIR?

426

GET THE PADDLE FROM YOUR COACH ONCE OR RUN LAPS FOR A WEEK?

427

BE A DOUBTING THOMAS OR DENY JESUS THREE TIMES LIKE PETER DID?

428

EAT PECAN PIE OR APPLE PIE?

429

430

HAVE A NORTHERN ACCENT OR A SOUTHERN DRAWL?

431

BE A SOUND ENGINEER OR A CAMERA OPERATOR?

432

BE A POSTAL WORKER OR A MICROBIOLOGIST?

433

BE BORED OR TOO BUSY?

434 DRILL FOR OIL OR DIG FOR GOLD?

435 HAVE AN EXTREME BODY/FACE MAKEOVER OR AN EXTREME HOME MAKEOVER?

436 LOSE THE FEELING IN YOUR ARMS OR IN YOUR LEGS?

437
**HAVE
YOUR HAIR
CATCH
ON FIRE
OR YOUR
EYES
DOUSED
WITH
TABASCO
SAUCE?**

BE THE CAT IN THE HAT OR THE
GRINCH WHO STOLE CHRISTMAS? 438

COMPOSE AN OPERA OR
CONDUCT A SYMPHONY? 439

SEE A BROADWAY PLAY OR READ
THE BOOK? 440

BE A STUNT DOUBLE FOR A
FAMOUS ACTOR OR HAVE SMALL 441
SPEAKING PARTS IN FAMOUS
MOVIES?

FLY A JET PLANE OR A TWIN
ENGINE PROP? 442

SHED YOUR SKIN LIKE A SNAKE
OR MOLT LIKE A BIRD? 443

CHASE A DANGEROUS CRIMINAL
THROUGH THE CITY OR IDENTIFY
A CRIMINAL THROUGH A SERIES
OF PHOTOGRAPHS? 444

GO THROUGH LIFE AS THE
ABSOLUTE TALLEST PERSON
IN HISTORY OR THE ABSOLUTE
SHORTEST? 445

446   HAVE A SOUR TASTE IN YOUR
MOUTH THAT WON'T GO AWAY OR
HEAR A CONSTANT RINGING IN
YOUR EARS?

DIRECT A MOVIE OR STAR IN ONE? 447

BE A GREAT SINGER OR A GREAT ACTOR? 448

DIE OF STARVATION OR OF THIRST? 449

SING A SOLO OR GIVE A SPEECH IN FRONT OF YOUR ENTIRE SCHOOL? 450

HAVE ONE CLOSE FRIEND OR A LOT OF ACQUAINTANCES? 451

LIVE IN AN EXCITING CITY OR A QUIET SUBURB? 452

BE RESPECTED OR POPULAR? 453

KNOW THE EXACT MOMENT OF YOUR DEATH FIVE YEARS FROM NOW OR DIE UNEXPECTEDLY ANYTIME BETWEEN ONE AND 10 YEARS FROM NOW? 454

BE AT JESUS' CRUCIFIXION OR AT THE LAST SUPPER?
455

456
BE AT THE EPICENTER OF AN EARTHQUAKE OR IN THE EYE OF A HURRICANE?

SKY DIVE OR DEEP-SEA DIVE?
457

PLAY IN THE NFL OR THE NBA?
458

SPEAK WITH GOD FOR ONE MINUTE OR ADD 10 YEARS TO YOUR LIFE?

459

HAVE YOUR NOSE HAIR PLUCKED
OR YOUR ARMPIT HAIR WAXED?

460

TAKE CARE OF FIVE ANIMALS OR
FIVE CHILDREN?

461

LISTEN TO OPERA OR COUNTRY
MUSIC?

462

EAT M&MS OR REESE'S PIECES?

463

464 LOOK OLDER THAN YOU ARE OR YOUNGER?

465 SPEND A SUMMER WITHOUT AIR CONDITIONING OR A WINTER WITHOUT HEAT?

RETAIL $29.99

EVERY PICTURE TELLS A STORY

48 EVOCATIVE PHOTOGRAPHS FOR INSPIRING REACTION AND REFLECTION

MARK OESTREICHER

INCLUDES LEADER'S GUIDE WITH 18 DIFFERENT USES FOR PERSONAL MEDITATION OR GROUP DISCUSSION

ISBN 0310241960

Teenagers are visual. From the fashions they wear to videos they watch, students make sense of the world based on what they see.

LET'S GIVE THEM SOMETHING VISUAL THAT WILL MAKE THEM THINK.

These 48 black-and-white photos, along with a leader's guide with 18 creative ways to use the photos in large or small groups, will help you inspire your students to react, reflect, pray, and share how the pictures speak to their souls.

www.youthspecialties.com/store

Youth Specialties